IN THE NINETEENTH CENTURY a famous naturalist called Humboldt believed that swallows hibernated for the duration of the winter months in the mud at the bottoms of ponds and marshy areas. People went on believing this for many years; they could not imagine that such tiny birds could fly more than one hundred and fifty miles a day in their long migration from Europe to the warm winters of South Africa – a total distance of over five thousand miles.

Swallow Journey

Vivian French

Illustrated by
Karin Littlewood

ZERO TO TEN

It is a quiet day in late April. The sun is hidden behind a haze of clouds, and there is little wind. The only sounds to break the silence are the rumble of a distant tractor and a twittering warble from high up on a telephone wire.

Old John looks up from his vegetable garden. He sees the bird and nods.

"Swallows are back," he says to himself. "Spring's here." And he goes on digging.

Up on the telephone wire the small bird with the long forked tail is no longer alone. Others have flown in to join him, and soon the wire is lined with swallows. Then, as if in answer to an invisible call, they leave the wire and fly down to the farm buildings below.

EACH SWALLOW KNOWS where it is going. The nests under the roof eaves are empty and waiting. There may be a pause in a wing beat, but the swallows only hesitate for a second or two. Skimmer heads for the milking shed. The building is only three years old, but there is a small gap between the front wall and the roof. Last year Skimmer and Sweet Claw built a new nest there. It is a deep bowl of mud mixed with saliva and grass which kept their eggs and babies safe and protected. Skimmer is going back home.

Skimmer takes possession of last year's nest. The mud has dried and cracked a little during the winter months, but the grass stems still bind it safely. He will not need to rebuild it. When Sweet Claw arrives to join Skimmer, she will replace the few feathers that remain from last year's lining.

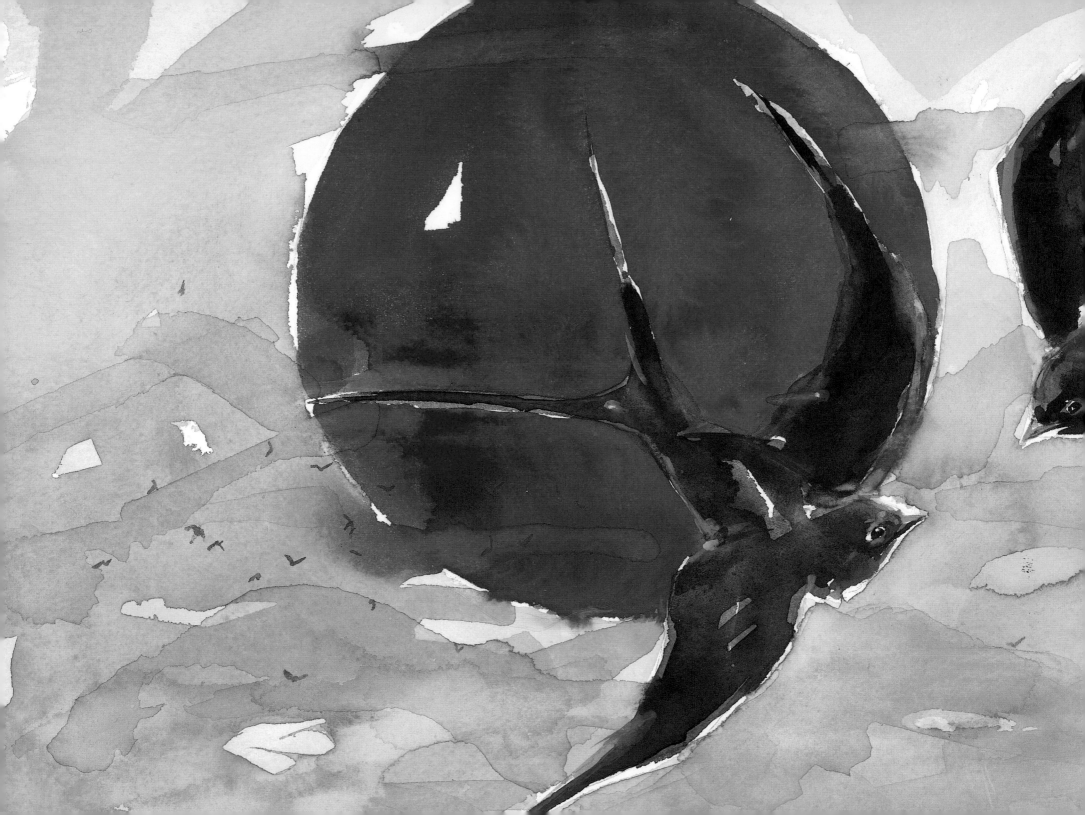

AS THE EVENING DRAWS IN and the sun sinks slowly behind the clouds, Skimmer swoops away from the milking shed and over and around the farmyard. Bluebottle flies are still buzzing about the heaps of dung and he flicks and zigzags to catch them. His forked tail spreads wide and then closes again, as he dips and dives to snap up fly after fly.

Sweet Claw flies in a day or so later. She travelled much of her journey north with other females, but as they crossed the English Channel, the flock began to break into fours and fives, then twos and threes. Sweet Claw arrives alone, and she banks above the farmyard and swings down to the milking shed to join Skimmer and their nest.

IN MAY, SWEET CLAW lays the last of her four red speckled eggs. Then, as the weather warms up, and only two weeks after the first egg was laid, movement and pushing come from inside it. A tiny naked chick squirms into the world, and Blue is born.

By the time Blue is nine days old, all the chicks have hatched and begun to grow feathers. Until they do, Sweet Claw does not leave them. They might have gotten cold and died without the warmth of her body. Now, she and Skimmer can take turns circling the farm and the area around in their never-ending search for food. Blue's yellow beak is always gaping open, and he pushes and jostles his brothers and sister in his eagerness to feed.

AS THE SUMMER GOES ON, Blue grows independent. He learns to fly strongly and no longer relies on Skimmer and Sweet Claw for food. He stays close to the nest, because there is another clutch of eggs now. When they hatch, Blue will help to feed the babies.

All too soon, the swallows gather again. August is not yet over, but groups of birds perch in twittering lines along the telephone wires. A third brood of babies is growing up in the nest, and Sweet Claw and Skimmer are still finding plenty of flies and other insects in the long hot dusty days. They seem in no hurry to leave, but though Blue still circles the farm, he grows increasingly restless.

Suddenly there is a cold spell. The leaves begin to turn from green to yellow and brown, and more and more swallows line the wires overhead. Sweet Claw and Skimmer, followed by four young fledglings, swoop out of the farmyard and join the throng. Blue is already there.

THE FLOCK LEAVES the following morning. No signal can be seen, but every bird flutters up into the air, wheels, and then turns to the South. Down below, Old John watches them. "There they go," he says. "Winter's on the way."

There is no one leader. As they fly, different birds move to the front while others fall back. Their flying speed, about fifteen miles per hour, helps the weaker birds. They are able to ride in the slipstream and save their strength; there is a long way to go. Blue exults in the regular beating of his blue-black wings. Something deep inside him has been longing for this flight, even though he has no way of knowing what lies at the other end.

DURING THE FIRST DAY, the swallows travel over one hundred and fifty miles. They cross the English Channel, and stop for the night on the edge of a village in northwest France. In a field, horses move around, and Blue and the other young swallows swoop down.

Small clouds of midges are dancing in the molten gold of the setting sun, and, by the time Blue settles himself to roost on the bare branches of an old tree, he is well fed.

As the days go on the swallows cross France and battle over the cold and bareness of the Pyrenees into Spain. Some birds do not make it; the younger, weaker birds do not have the strength to fight against the wind and lack of food.

Blue swoops and circles when the sun sets; he sinks down near Skimmer and Sweet Claw to sleep until the dawn breaks and it is time to fly yet again.

ON AND ON AND ON fly the swallows. Down through eastern Spain they go, always heading south. Although there are now many insects in the air, and it is not difficult to feed, the sun is strangely hot on Blue's back and he tires in the unfamiliar warmth. The flying is easier when land turns to sea and a cooling wind begins to blow.

The northwest wind begins to blow harder now. It catches at the crest of the waves and white spray tosses high into the air. The swallow leaders soar up and swoop down the wind's back. Blue, now at the tail end of a wide V strung across the sky, is caught unawares by the blustering and flutters wildly. Then he too catches the strength of the wind under his wings, and for one glorious moment sweeps and swings effortlessly towards the coast line of North Africa.

THE SAHARA IS VAST. There are hot winds, and shifting sands. Food is scarce, and water holes are few and far between. Blue beats on. The flock is smaller now, but still, when the winds allow it, they keep to the same speed. They have been travelling for three weeks, but crossing the desert is the hardest test of all.

Blue is flying behind Sweet Claw. Suddenly, a twist of wind catches at a hill of sliding sand and tosses it up and into the air. Blue and Sweet Claw can see nothing but shimmering and blinding glitter. They blunder on, lurching and dipping, unable to see and unable to breathe. Sweet Claw falls first, then Blue. They lie half stifled, flapping and scrabbling at the suffocating sand that blows all around them.

A SMALL GENTLE HAND lifts Sweet Claw, then Blue, dusts
them down, and places them in the cool of a tent wall.
It leaves a little water, and then leaves them alone,
hunched in the shade.

As the wind dies Sweet Claw begins to stir.
"So, my pretty ones," says a voice. "Are you ready to fly?"
The gentle hand comes again, and Sweet Claw feels herself
tossed up into the warm, still air. Blue soon follows, and
together they fly up and away. By evening they have found
the straggling flyers at the back of their migrating flock.

THE SWALLOWS LEAVE THE SAHARA BEHIND. As the first green bushes and shrubs come into view, Blue flies down and around in a circle. There are many insects; a group of wildebeest have fed and stayed overnight nearby, and flies are buzzing and humming around their droppings. The swallows feed hungrily, but they cannot stay for long. They still hear the call, and they cannot stop, yet.

Six weeks after the swallows left England, they are still flying. But something is different; the urgency is gone. Blue circles and swoops and dives, and seems to be in no hurry. Small groups of birds break away from the main flock.

Sweet Claw and Skimmer head towards a cluster of little houses, and the fields of cattle belonging to the village. Blue follows them.

DOWN BELOW A WOMAN is tending to
her crops. She looks up, and sees the wave
of swallows as they fly above her.
"What are those?" asks a child beside her.
"Swallows," says her mother.
The child stares at the birds.
"Are they here to stay?"
"No," says her mother. "Just until March,
or so." She puts down her basket
and waves at another worker.
"Hey! Swallows are back!"

Blue swoops in a circle, and catches a fly.

For Ella, with love – V.F.

For Lucy – K.L.

First published in 2001 by Zero To Ten Limited
814 North Franklin Street, Chicago, Illinois 60610
and 327 High Street, Slough, Berkshire, SL1 1TX, UK

Publisher: Anna McQuinn
Art Director: Tim Foster
Senior Editor: Simona Sideri
Publishing Assistant: Vikram Parashar

Library of Congress CIP data applied for.

ISBN 1-84089-215-3

Printed in Hong Kong

ABP1448

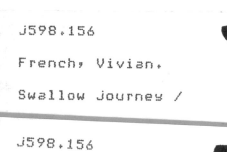
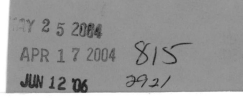